At Sula's Feet
by Ersula Knox Odom

~ Foreward ~

A very shy college student came home for the summer, sat down at her grandmother's feet and said "tell me the stories you used to tell me". Since her grandmother adored her, she granted her wish. She spent the afternoon singing, laughing, and sharing with her grand daughter the moments that would create an abundance of goodwill throughout the years to come. The moments that would be needed to prove to her great grand children just how wonderful she was. They recorded the voice that would delight her aging daughter some 30 years later. She shared information that would reveal the personality traits that were repeated generation after generation. They recorded a moment in time to be shared with her family who would later miss her. That student was me- Ersula Knox Odom.

    The tape recorder was huge and malfunctioned. I was distressed at having my tight, reserved voice recorded along with the clear strong voice of my hero. But something within me refused to stop. I knew then that these stories would be a part of me forever. I had no idea HOW MUCH.

    Since I was raised by a grandmother who was the youngest and last surviving sister of seven brothers and sisters. I was perfectly placed to enjoy family history. Everyone came to visit his or her good-natured auntie. Affording me opportunities to enjoy those endearing walks down memory lane. Each relative having a slightly different and fascinating twist to the same stories. These experiences and my enthusiasm for collecting such information, later earned me the title of family historian.

    In fact it appears my past actions were setting the stage and lying dormant until I matured enough to truly be excited about revealing the past to the future.

    I kept scrapbooks in high school. Became the self appointed

photographer for the theatre department in college. Kept a journal during college including as an exchange student in London. Kept letters written to me during college. I exchanged audiotapes, at my request, instead of letters with my high school boy friend. We were separated by different college choices. Retrieved old photos from Grandmother shortly before the family home was destroyed by fire. Recorded my paternal grandmother reciting a birthday poem to my maternal grandmother for her 90th birthday. Begged my aunt to go into the attic of her house, which was about to be sold, to "see" if there was "anything" up there. We rescued generations of history that had been packed away and forgotten. I spent hours searching through census records for family connections and documenting my findings for our family reunions. I informally preserve special events and milestones from my career. I am a historian by birth, recently spent my birthday in a scrap booking class with my daughters. My friends now label me as a "story teller".

In 2001 following a college reunion I was driven to use today's technology to organize it all and prepare for collecting more. All forms of collecting family history appeal to me, including oral history. It is comforting to know that these "life lyrics," building family trees, organizing photos, following people around with a microphone and writing stories will ensure that I will never be bored nor our history lost.

Ersula~

~ Acknowledgments ~

To Knox, Smarty, and Odom Families am you.

Especially Rosie, Danielle, Osborne,
Margaret, Walter, Bobby & Annette,
Jackie & Doug, Gladys, Deborrah,
Retta & Sutton, Betty & Sonny, Johnnie, Roberta,
Willie & Charlene, Bernard and Ronald.

Friends Through it All

Herbert, Nay, Robert, Michael, Donna, Betty, Kermit,
Richedean, Tanya, Brenda & Arthur, Willie & Emma,
Carl & Shelia, Waymon & Jackie, Maria,
Ali, Maurice & Mryna, Uwezo,
St John Progressive's Choir #3, The Jaguars, Sharks,
Knockouts, Hounds and Dream Team.

Special thanks to

Felecia Wintons and Ricc Rollins for a dream fulfilling
birthday present
and to Lorenzo Robertson for
dotting the i's and crossing the t's.

and lastly to you....

Yes your name should be here
If we have met we have had an impact
on each other's lives.
We took a moment in time to become
a part of each other's history.
I thank you for sharing a part of yourself,
such that I can be who I am.

To my Angels:
Ursula Stephens, Gladys Knox, Janie Shellman,
Jessie Reese, Alta Harvey, Ella Fisher & Cousin Pleasant-
I dedicated this book to you...

With all my love
Ersula

Let the journey begin....

Table of Contents

Foreward vii
Acknowledgments ix
Dedication xi

~ Simply a Way of Life ~

A Washboard and Twisted Coat Hanger 3
Corn Rows 4
First Garden Competition 5
Foot Tub Bath 6
Hair in Bird's Nest 7
Learning to Braid 8
No Comments Allowed 9
Outdoor Toilet 10
Sleeping in the Window 11
Behind the Plow 12
Snakes 13
On Another Day 14
Last Night Home 15
The Brothers (Black Men in the 50's) 16
Tin Roof 17
Wooden Church Floor - Heel Music 18

~ Food for My Soul ~

Black Berry Doobie 21
Last Black Berry Doobie 22
Breakin' It Down 23
Church Picnics & Checkerboard Cakes 24
The Brothers (Black Men in the 50's) 25
Oranges From Florida 26
Eating Clay 27
The Heart of the Watermelon 28
Sweet Potato Bank 29
The Rolling Store Man 30
We At Staples 31
We Dunked Biscuits 32
Yahoo Mountain Dew - Shake 33

~ Sula: My Amazing Grace ~

Black Grandmother 37
So Which One is it? U or E? 38
Sula 39
What Happened to My Name 40
Self Motivation 41
Grandmother's Opinon 42
Caring 43
Life's Dirty Joke 44
Limits of Love 45
Sleeping with Grandmama 46
Bearable Grief 47
Plum Tree Switches 48
Caught with the Cigarettes 49
The Preacher's Voice 50
I Saw You 51

~ Working It! ~

Iron Wash Pot 55
Milking a Cow 56
Making Butter 57
Mr. Ed's Tobacco Farm 58
Priming the Pump 59

Later Moments

Nay 63
The Names you Call Me 64
The Wind 65
The Way to My Heart 66
You're Different 67
Lady Justice 68
Mental Homeless Jailbird 69

Entertaining Ourselves

Call to play 73
Dancing 74
Footsteps on the Porch 75
Going Fishing 76
Grown Folks Conversation 77

Our Story 78
Sugar Girl: Country Girl Goes North 79
Ponies, Horses and Mules: Pony 80
Ponies, Horses and Mules: Horse 81
Ponies, Horses and Mules: Mule 82
The Roast 83
Swinging on a Tree Limb 84
Watching the Radio 85

~ Support System ~

Inspiration Just Walked In 88
Bible Under My Pillow 89
Discipline One: Spank Her 90
Discipline One: The Agreement 91
Church on Sunday 92
Good Bye Auntie 93
Mentally Ill Mom 94
Nice Words 96
Nosey Neighbor 97
Oh the Shame of it All 98
Outcast's Companion 99
Secrets 100
The Baby Child 101
The Sanctified Church 102
Luv Ya 103
My Father's Name 104
My Mother's Name 105

~ Final Thought ~

Brain Washing 108
Greetings that Matter 110
That's Life 111
Life's a Journey 112
Misunderstood 113
Motivation 114
Selfish 115
Sweet Potato Bank 2 116
You Folks 117
Baby Shower 118
Born with It 120

~Simply a Way of Life~

Ursula Knox Odom

"Sula, you ain't got no sense"
"Oh, hush up Jessie!"
Typical banter between Grun'mama & Grandaddy

At Sula's Feet

A Wash Board and Twisted Hanger

"Cleanliness is next to Godliness"
Maybe your duel role
Inspired this blessedness

On wash day
Rub-a-dub Rub-a-dub
to clean our clothes

On Sunday
Chey-chey-chey-chey
Chey-chey-chey-chey
to clean our hearts

The music you made
Lifted our voices to heaven
And delivered our souls to God

Ersula Knox Odom

Corn Rows - the One With Ears

Corn rows in the field
Corn rows in my hair

One made me feel good
One made me look good

Many hours were spent
Weaving in and out
Of the tall green stalks
With ears of corn

Many hours were spent
Weaving corn rows of hair
Of this tall brown girl
With ears adorn.

At Sula's Feet

First Garden Competition

No matter how often I visited them
No matter how often I talked to them
No matter how often I prayed about them
The darn things just didn't grow

They needed fertilizer
From a bag or from a horse
The choice was for the wiser

Barry's dad knew

Barry took such pleasure
As his vegetable garden grew
Bigger and bigger
Into his treasure

To Barry's delight
My pewney little leaves
And pewney little potatoes
Was such a sorry sight.

Ersula Knox Odom

Foot Tub Bath

Taking a bath in a foot tub
Under a pot belly stove
Its smokey red pipes bending towards the ceiling
In a sideways "S"

I lifted my arms to reach my back
And my elbow met
With that ever so shocking stove pipe
Which seemed its hottest yet.

Ouch.
As if once wasn't enough
I repeated this moment
Far too many times

Now my elbow has a smooth round spot
As a life long token of our union

At Sula's Feet

Hair In Bird's Nest

What - Comb your hair outside?
What - Sweep your hair outside?
What - Clean your comb outside?

What ever could be the matter with you?

You must be crazy
Or crazy you will be

For a bird will build
A nest with your hair
And crazy you will be

Ursula Knox Odom

Learning to Braid

Thank you Barbara
For letting me practice on you
For being my human mannequin

I would have used a doll
But there were none with hair like ours

Sorry
That I braided it so thin
That Ms Lonon had to undo it with a key

You're welcome
For the tale you can tell
Until you are old and grey

At Sula's Feet

No Comments Allowed

Sex Education
Dogs
Chickens
Horses
Bulls

Death
Horse Trails
    (Stiff horses dragged down the road)
Buzzards
    (That's how they found her)
Hogs & Chicken
    (They eat chickens alive ya' know)
Bambi hit by a car
    (There was something not right about that)
Puppies chasing cars
    (Mr. Saxon - hated for life -"you killed my dog")

Ersula Knox Odom

Outdoor Toilet

As you crossed the threshold
To the outdoor throne

You had to look up
To see if a snake was on the door ledge

You tried not to look down
Into this deep hole in the ground
Upon the squirmy, wiggly,
All natural, waste eliminating
Maggots below

At Sula's Feet

Sleeping in the Window

Do you know what it feels like?
Have you ever done it?

Ursula Knox Odom

Behind The Plow

Much like driving the first time
The first time behind a plow
Was a long awaited privilege
The very act of placing your
Hands on the plow handles
Brought uncontrollable giggles
With handles at shoulder level
It was uncertain who was really in control
The littlest driver or the mule
The sound of giggles however
Was quickly over taken
By the sound of Granddaddy's laughter
For he had not seen
A funnier sight in a many a days

At Sula's Feet

Snakes

One day
A king snake befriended Grandmama
He bump bumped her heal
She tossed him away
To save his life
For him to kill a rattlesnake
On some other day

He bump bumped her heal again
She tossed again
He bumped again
She tossed again

Then
She ended it all.

It must have bothered her
For she told us about him
Time and time again

Ersula Knox Odom

On Another Day

Three grown women
(Roberta, Janie, Margaret)
Safe and sound
Within the confines of a car

Stopped the car
Got out
To kill a rattle snake
As he crossed the road

"Why" I asked
"Because he could hurt somebody"
They replied

At Sula's Feet

Last Night Home

There was a huge fire to light the night
Creating a large circle of light
Surrounded by darkness

For as I prepared to slay the ignorant dragon

My uncles celebrated the sight of their slain 7-foot rattle snake

What an appropriate trophy

They proclaimed it to be the biggest rattle-snake-kill of the season

True or not
I still see this long, fat, lifeless snake
Hanging from the smoke house

I still hear the joy and excitement
Radiating from that soft glow out back

This moment gave us all something to focus on
Besides packing up my belongings to leave home for good

No longer a child

The men had done their job
They had done the he-man-thing with the snake

The women had done their job
I was off to college

Now
It was up to me

Ersula Knox Odom

The Brothers (Black Men in the 50s)

They were clean
They looked like money
So handsome
In their silky suits
Draping their silky skin

To look at the picture the world was perfect
You mess with one you mess with them all
If only the world treated them
As good as they looked

God truly had a good time making them
His paint brush just glided over his human canvas
Producing those
Sparkling eyes
Glistening smiles
Oh you slender molds of perfection

At Sula's Feet

Tin Roof

The lights went out
Appliances unplugged
Bed covers pulled back
Family members retreated

To their favorite spot in bed

To listen to the soothing sound of
Rain hitting that tin roof

No better warmth
No better sleep
No better respect for nature's power

Ursula Knox Odom

Wooden Church Floor - Heel Music

Listen
Can you hear it?

tap-clap, tap-clap...
tap-clap, tap-clap...
tap-clap, tap-clap...
tap-clap, tap-clap...
tap-clap, tap-clap...
tap-clap, tap-clap...

clap-clap-tap, clap-clap-tap...
clap-clap-tap, clap-clap-tap...
clap-clap-tap, clap-clap-tap...
clap-clap-tap, clap-clap-tap...

At Sula's Feet

~ Food for My Soul ~

Ursula Knox Odom

*"Preparing food was a labor of love.
She even faught snakes as long as she could
to get the blue berries for doobie"*

At Sula's Feet

Black Berry Doobie

We risked a whipping
We risked our love ones lives

All in pursuit of the blackberries & blueberries
For that wonderful doobie

Biscuit dough soaked up
Swee-eeet flavor and royal blue color
As they bounced around in a sea of berry juice

Grandmama told my cousin (Anita) and me
"Don't go over in that field" [to pick berries]
But Granddaddy was going
So we rationalized that
He would keep us safe.

He did from nature
But not from Grandmama.

This slender woman met us with a 6 foot switch
She advanced with such determination
You could see the word CHARGE!!!
Written on her forehead.

Anita went left
 I went right
Granddaddy was stuck in the middle
Holding the reigns of the horse
Because it was better to be whipped as a child
Than chase a runaway wagon.

Ersula Knox Odom

Last Blue Berry Doobie

That day pails by comparison to
The day Grandmama announced
"I'm tired of fighting those snakes for blueberries"

That's when I knew snakes were truly evil
For they were the reason
We had had our last Blueberry doobie.

At Sula's Feet

Breakin' It Down

For you it is a BLT

Without the lettuce
A bacon sandwich

Without the bacon
A tomato sandwich

Without the tomato
A mayonnaise sandwich

For me

Ursula Knox Odom

Church Picnics & Checkerboard Cake

Checkerboard cake, potato salad and fried chicken

There is something special about
Eating chicken and cake together

Miss Sweetie Mae
How did you make
Your checker board cake?

She simply would smile or maybe nod
But never did she say.

At Sula's Feet

How Do You Like Your Grits

With scrambled eggs, salt & pepper and lil' hot sauce
With smothered pork chop
With gravy
With cheese please
No cheese just butter will do
With an over easy egg on top please
With a little butter is just fine for me
With pork sausage mixed in please
With red-eye gravy if you don't mind

Any way but gritty- ookkay!

What you mean you don't
Serve fish for breakfast!!

Fish-n-grits
Is for dinner, supper
And breakfast too

Ersula Knox Odom

Oranges From Florida

When the word got out that Cousin Charlie had arrived from Florida with a trunk full of oranges, excitement filled the air

Our Florida cousin with the South Carolina voice was home

So simple to do
Yet it raised him to a level of family celebrity

At Sula's Feet

Eating Clay

Why did she do that?

Ersula Knox Odom

Sweet Potato Bank

Dug a hole deep and wide
Lined it with pine needle straw
Filled it with sweet potatoes
Covered it with straw
Covered it with dirt

Rain water kept the potatoes clean
Straw kept them dry
The ground kept them cool

No chemicals
No refrigerator
No hurry

They remain harvest fresh
From one harvest to the next

Throughout the year
The potatoes patiently waited
For a hand to part the dirt
Wide enough for
A hand to get in
And a potato to get out.

At Sula's Feet

The Heart of the Water Melon

When plucked from the vine
On a hot summer day,

The seedless heart
soooo cold
Oh soooo sweet.

Ersula Knox Odom

The Rolling Store Man.

You must have enjoyed you fate in life
Bringing joy to those
Farm family souls

What a thrill to say
Grandmama, Granddaddy
The Rolling Store Man is Here!!!

Spices for Grandmama
Sweets for me
A can of Prince Albert for Granddaddy

Ohh...Wait..... A..... Minute

The last time that you came
You delighted us with shrimp

I ate a pound all... by... myself
Then I got sick all...by..myself

At Sula's Feet

We Ate Staples

Even though I used them everyday
It took me a while
To realize
An office supply store named - Staples
Was really - a good idea.

I had to think twice

Because where I come from
Staples meant
Flour
Grits
&
Rice.

Ersula Knox Odom

We Dunked Biscuits

People say it
But I never see them do it

They got it wrong anyway
You don't dunk donuts
You dunk biscuits

The cream and sugar were in the coffee
Not the bread
Donuts just to sweet to cut it

For coffee
Sugar to sweeten it
Biscuits to soak it
Cream to mellow it

With Donuts they sip It

At Sula's Feet

Yahoo Mountain Dew - Shake

They arrived in big trucks
Making lots of noise
Having lots of fun

Those tree climbing
Men with loud voices

The words "mountain dew"
And pecans falling that sound like rain
Will forever be connected in my brain

It was the first time
I had heard either

From their separate, self selected, tree limbs

The men yelled
Yahoo!! Mountain Dew!!

In unison the men jumped
And down came the pecans
like rain.

Ursula Knox Odom

"Why You Pointin' that thing at Me?"

Sula on our one and only photoshoot
-1973

At Sula's Feet

~Sula: My Amazing Grace~

Ersula Knox Odom

"Everybody and everything wanted some of Gran'mama's time... and they always got it."

At Sula's Feet

Black Grandmother

Lost your child
Only to see that child's face
Everyday
In your grand-baby's face

Such pain - such joy

You no longer have
Your child to share
Day to day moments
But you share past good times with your grand-baby

Such pain - such joy

You feel so old
For you thought
Your child rearing days were done

You feel so young
For your grand-baby
Keeps you moving

Such pain - such joy

You feel so ignorant
For your grand-baby
Is speaking of things of which you know nothing

You feel so wise
For the basic lessons are still the same
As you pass them
On to your grand-baby

Such pain - such joy

Ersula Knox Odom

So Which One Is It ...U or E?

Sometimes she wrote it as Ursula
Sometimes Ersula
Why I asked?
She replied
She didn't like making the U
Realized that an E sounds the same
Concluded that if it sounds the same
It didn't much matter which one she used

When I came along
Someone must have said "Ursula with an E"
Thus my name became Eursula
I had to correct that
Ersula it is
To save my child from a life time
Of spelling and explaining her name
I spelled it Ursula
Her first monogrammed baby gift was spelled with an E
Oh well

At Sula's Feet

Sula

Cousin Willie addressed the congregation with such pride
She said:
"I have the pleasure of introducing
The mother of the church
The president of the missionary society
The president of the senior choir
The class leader of Sunday School class # ....
Our honoree- Mrs. URSULA Stephens
OH MY GOD!! Cousin Willie called my name.

Why did she do That!! I'm only 6 years....
OH MY GOODNESS!!!

Grandmama stood up
She's walking to the front
With a big smile on her face
Wait a minute!

My word, Grandmama's name is Ersula too!!!
That was the first time I heard anyone call her anything but SULA.
All these years I had only heard
Grandma Sula
An Sula
Cousin Sula
Miss Stev'n
Miss Sula
And just plain Sula

Oh I get it! Er......Sula!!!!

Ersula Knox Odom

What Happened To My Name?

To me
Grandmama called

Janie
Leola
Roberta
Margaret

Gal! Come here!

At Sula's Feet

Self Motivation

My first & middle names are Ersula Unice

Ersula means little she bear
I must be the epitome of strength
Yet gentle with those
Who treat me well

I am named for my grandmother
Ursula Smart Stephens
She was Ursa Major
I'm Ursa Minor
She was the big dipper
I'm the little dipper

Grandmother was the best in her league
I must strive to be the best in mine

My maiden name was Knox
Scottish for one who lives on a hill

I must place myself
In a position to see all that approaches
To make the best decision
At any given moment

Self preservation means
That when all else fails
Motivation is best
When it comes from within

Ersula Knox Odom

Grandmother's Opinion

You had your opinion
But you kept it to yourself

I asked:
"What happened between Mama & Daddy?"
You said:
"Ask your ma"

I asked:
"What happened between Mama & Daddy?"
You said:
"Ask your pa"

You had your opinion
But you kept it to yourself
I found out for myself
But devoid of hate

Because
You kept your opinion to yourself

At Sula's Feet

Caring

I was heartbroken when I was told
Of my last childhood puppy's pending motherhood
Fathered by a dog 10 times her size

Even though I was a sophomore in college
Home for the summer
I cried like a baby
For I just knew
That it was certain death for Candy

Uncle Johnnie laughed

Grandmama came to the rescue as usual
And said
"God has a way of taking care of these things"

Years later in hearing of Candy
My new husband named our new puppy Canti

Yesterday I was asked what was the end of the story
To my horror I had to admit
"I don't know"

I was comforted by Grandmother
And that was enough

I cared about Candy
But apparently not enough

Ersula Knox Odom

Life's Dirty Joke

The only dirty joke that Grandmama told me
Was no joke at all
For when she got married
She had never real...ly seen a man
She thought it was funny
So she laughed

She got pregnant - had twins
She got pregnant again - had twins

She said when she got pregnant a third time
She stopped laughing

At Sula's Feet

Limits of Love

I said:
Grandmama I love you so much
I don't think that I could stand it
If you died before me

She said: Uh huh

I said:
Grandmama I love you so much
I don't think that I could stand it
If you died before me

She said: Uh huh

I said:
Grandmama I love you so much
I don't think that I could stand it
If you died before me

She said:
You know—
If you really mean that
God is a good God and He answer prayers
If you pray He'll hear you

I thought:
She's 68 and I'm 10
I said: Uh huh

Ersula Knox Odom

Sleeping with Grandmama

As we slept
She made me feel warm
She made me feel safe
She made me feel loved

As we formed this human chair in bed

Today
As a mother of girls
That I love
I now know

I made her feel warm, safe and loved

At Sula's Feet

Bearable Grief

I often wonder
How you could bear so much pain
You watched
Your son of 16 years
Your son of your second set of twins
Die
A slow death
From a broken back
Others said
Your favorite brother was the cause
You simply said
"he hurt his back over in in the fields"
You watched your daughter inhale
The flames from her burning dress
Others speak of her
You quietly revive the memory of
This child named for
Your mother and your mother-in-law
Your unborn baby
Lost
In the midst of your grief
For your daughter
Others say eight
You simply said to me
"I had nine"

Ursula Knox Odom

Plum Tree Switches

"Go get me a switch!! She screamed
What a cruel thing to make me do

For my fate
Was determined by
The fate
Of that skinny little plum tree branch

If she was angry she said "Gal I'll kill you"
Yet she gave me some slack
For she used that skinny little branch
With all its leaves in tack

If she was mad she said "Gal I'll kill you"
Now this was no dare
For she used that Skinny little branch
With it's leaves stripped bare

At Sula's Feet

Caught With the Cigarettes

Oh Dear I dropped them!

All I wanted to do
Was see what it was like
To smoke a cigarette.
My trip behind the pecan tree
Proved to be a terrible event

I gagged
I coughed
I hated it

Oh Dear I dropped them
And all I wanted to do was
Sneak those awful things
Back to the house

As I passed by Grandmama...
OH DEAR!! I DROPPED THEM!!
Then I heard
"What is it you got there?"

Who knows what happened next
I went into mental shock
For I had been caught with the cigarettes.

Ersula Knox Odom

The Preacher's Voice

Cousin Preacher was his name,
Cousin Pleasant was his wife
Thunder was the sound of his voice
That would put James Earl Jones to shame.

Cousin Preacher's voice was as clear and sharp as a bell.
His laughter filled the church.

Yet,
The voice was so soft
At Grandmama's funeral

It was as if all the joy was gone
Not only for Cousin Preacher

But for all of us who loved
And learned at Sula's Feet

At Sula's Feet

I Saw You!

How stupid could I be
"Grandmama I saw you"

In the wee hours of the night
With the warm glow
Of the Christmas tree light

Christmas came and went
Santa came and went
Christmas came and went
Santa came and went

In the wee hours of the night
With the warm glow
Of the Christmas tree light
The number of gifts did grow

But this night
As she eased back into bed
I said: "Grandmama, I saw you"
She said: "Good"

That was the last time
Santa came and went

Ersula Knox Odom

"Lord where Y'all taking my child!"
*Sula as we traveled to Eckerd College
across the Howard Franklin Bridge"*
~1972

At Sula's Feet

~ Working It! ~

Ursula Knox Odom

"Work was not a thing of discussion. From the field to Church, it just got done and with a smile."

Sula's philosophy on work & life.

At Sula's Feet

Iron Wash Pot

It was the way of the south
Every thing
And every body
Could do more than one thing

One day in the back yard
You boiled and boiled
To make soap from lye and lard

Another day in the back yard
You boiled and boiled
To clean our clothes
With soap made from lye and lard

Ersula Knox Odom

Milking a Cow

Vick, short for Victoria
Was our never ending milk factory.

She had one horn up
And one horn down

She responded to Grandmama
But had no patience for
Inexperienced children like me

She kicked
And fear sent us flying
She had no chance
Of reaching us at all

For she was framed by a wooden stall

PS: Was it love
Or was it Grandmama's sense of humor
To name her cows
After her sister [Sarah]
And sister-in-law [Victoria]

At Sula's Feet

Making Butter

We milked the cow
Allowed the milk to sit for awhile
The cream did rise to the top
Skimmed the cream off the top
Into a jar it was placed
Wrapped in a towel
Balanced on a knee

Rock-rock rock-rock
see-saw see-saw
Rock-rock rock-rock

Just when I felt
I could not rock
That jar another time
Out of nowhere formed a little clump of butter
Then another an another
Soon a hugh ball of butter
Would float to the top
Leaving weak looking skim milk behind

A little salt
A little kneading
A lot of flavor

The Mason jar wrapped in a towel
Was not the only way
But it was our way

Ursula Knox Odom

Mr. Ed's Tobacco Farm

Only the big kids could work
Why?
Was it that they got high
From inhaling the smoke
Of that mystery crop
With it's large wide leaves

Was it You Mr. Ed
That would not let me in
Or
Grandmama that would not let me go?

At Sula's Feet

Priming the Pump

Hiss-hiss-hiss

Now why was it so hard for me
To rid this pump of air

Why did the water I poured
Ran as fast as it could
To join the water below

When Grandmama did it
The water rushed up the pipe
To greet her

Ersula Knox Odom

"Get old or die young"
Sula on people not wanting to reveal their age

At Sula's Feet

~ Later Moments ~

Ursula Knox Odom

Nay!

Reached back to the past
Reached forward to the future

I am sure I was your number one fan

You had no faults
For those you did I ignored

You were all knowing
And anointed with God-given talent

You spoke
We gazed
You sang
We praised

My goodness
How smart
How talented
How compassionate you were.

At Sula's Feet

The Names You Call Me

Velvet

Bon Chocolat

Nubian Beauty

[Smooth, Black, Sweet, Tall, Beauty]

Ersula Knox Odom

The Wind

Sitting - Thinking about you.

Something drifted around my shoulders,
I turned around and discovered
That it was only the wind.

Dismayed I continued daydreaming.

Something whipped around my waist,
I looked around (smiling),
Nothing,
The wind again.

I stretched out on my stomach,
Closed my eyes and something tickled my feet,
I laughed,
Opened my eyes....
My heart sank,
The wind again.

Then Revelation!!!

It was you all the time.

Your love is so strong and
My reception so sharp that
Even the wind brings your love to me.

At Sula's Feet

The Way To My Heart

I write this
Not because I believe it poetic
Not because I believe it cute
Not because I think that it fits

I write this because I want the world to know
How much you mean to me
And for you to see just how serious I am about it

To Nay, I survived college academically
Because I turned in my assignments
I survived emotionally because of you
The thought of sharing life lessons
In our golden years
Is like extending the beauty
Of a sunset for eternity

To Herbert, In all the years since we met
You have never missed a birthday
If everyone else ignored me
You gave me one small thing to look forward to
The occasional phone call where your voice
Became a most precious thing

To both of you- thank you
For laughing at me and with me
For taking me seriously and crying with me
For sharing you with me
For being my friends for life

Ersula Knox Odom

You're Different

The defensive side of me says
To fear you

The curious side of me
Is fascinated by you
And wants to know why

The intellectual side of me
Understands
That you have that right

The political side of me says
To betray you

The weak side of me
Is embarrassed by you

The cowardly side of me
Fails to defend you

The pristine side of me
Loves you for who you are

At Sula's Feet

Lady Justice

She may be blind
But she can smell your money

She may be blind
But she can hear your language

She may be blind
But she can feel your hair

To be treated justly by Lady Justice

You have to
Have the right hair
Speak her language
And have money.

Ersula Knox Odom

Mental-Homeless-Jailbird

The tour guide said
"A large number of street people are mentally ill."

I commented to the prison guide
"It appears a lot of these people are mentally ill."
He said "you're right"

I wonder
Why is this better

Maybe
It releases government from
    Medical cost
    Housing cost
    Social service cost
It releases family
    From caring physically
    From emotional involvement
    From reality

Back up!!
    In jail they get food, housing
    For life...
    It's not about cost
    It's about dignity

At Sula's Feet

Wit doms on making excuses

Patricia:
"Well Grandmama, I better get going before it gets dark."

Sula said with a chuckle:
"What? Your car don't have lights?"

Ersula Knox Odom

"Life was a special occasion in our family"

At Sula's Feet

~ Entertaining Ourselves ~

Ursula Knox Odom

"Our connection to the a world outside Route 2, Box One Eleven"

At Sula's Feet

Call to Play

The telephone may have made life easier
But it certainly wasn't as much fun.

You whisper

We screamed:

Baaaaaa Reeee!!!
Can you come out and play???!!!

Ersssssss Laaaa!!!
Can you come out and play??!!!

Meeettt Meee Hallff Wayyyyy!

Ersula Knox Odom

Dancing

The me that is too shy to be spoken
Comes alive on stage

As my body says

I love life
I love me
I want you to love me

But I'm afraid to say

So I'll leave it to imagine

At Sula's Feet

Footsteps on the Porch

The greatest joy
Of an only child's day
Is the sound of
A new child with which to play.

Shelia Tyson
Your footsteps are forever
Planted in my mind

Boom, Boom, Bang!!!

Two steps on the porch
Through the screen door.

What Joy!!!

You, my new neighbor
Was in my house.

Ersula Knox Odom

Going Fishing

I would follow my uncle anywhere
But on this day
I feared my judgment was elsewhere

There was that horrible sound again
"Uncle Johnny?!" I cried
He replied:
"Gal, those gators don't want you"

With mud up to my knee
I had to believe Uncle John-ny
Was as right as right could be

For there was no guarantee
The gators would agree
Not to make a meal out of me

At Sula's Feet

Grown Folks Conversation

Being seen and not heard
Was fine by me
For then I could hear every word
Of the grown folks talk

Cousin this and cousin that
Her child, his child, whose child

He left her
She left the church

The preacher this
And the preacher that

Sister M this
And Sister R that

What you say?
Oh no, I missed that

Ersula Knox Odom

"Our Story"

"Our Story is on" yelled Shelia's little sister
To ensure that we didn't miss
A single moment of our favorite soap opera.

"We will return to our story in just a moment,"
 the announcer would say
Permitting us to momentarily resume some childish play.

At Sula's Feet

Sugar Girl - Country Girl Goes North

What cold white wonder is this

"Grandma, Grandma
It's raining sugar"

From this point on
I was to be known
"The Sugar Girl"

Ersula Knox Odom

Ponies, Horses and Mules: Pony

Wow a pony
Just my size
I would get to ride a beautiful Shetland pony
But wait
I had nothing to hold on to but his mane

With my legs in a death grip around his belly
My head inched closer
And closer to land
Finally it took it's place in the sand
Off that pony went in full gait

It took some time
For my uncles to catch that pony
His victory and new found freedom
He was determined to celebrate

At Sula's Feet

Ponies, Horses and Mules: Horse

I watched you from my window
As you enjoyed your freedom and reward
From your racing career

To Uncle Johnnie's delight
You ran faster when they pulled the reigns
Trying to stop you
You came to a dead stop as they gave the command
Even they did not understand
Tossing these young boys that would not listen

My fascination got the best of me
And yes I ventured out onto your playground
You were thrilled and ran around like a giant puppy
And then up to me at full speed to greet me, stood straight up
Leaving only your belly for me to see

As this rising waterfall of Mahogany flesh
loomed above me
I knew that I could not move
If I could not see your eyes
You could not see me
Yet you knew where I was
I knew to leave it at that

Ersula Knox Odom

Ponies, Horses and Mules: Mule

Your work was long and hard
Leading medal, wood and man

You led the
Plow to split the earth
So that corn, peanuts, and potatoes
Would have some place to grow

You led the wagon taking us to the field
The store, a neighbors house
And to church

On your days off

You enjoyed
The warm legs on your old bones
The warmest in your heart
Of the giggling little ones
Taking their first "horseback" ride.

At Sula's Feet

The Roast

Standing before a fireplace
On a cold winter night

I Stretched out my hand
Palm to heat
I Stretched out my hand
Palm to me

Caught the heat
And sent it through my body

Drew close to warm
The front half of my body
Turned around to baste the back

Just as I turned warm and toasty

Some fun loving jokester
Pulled my pants tight
Turning aaahh to ouch!!!
And toasted to burnt.

Ursula Knox Odom

Swinging on a tree limb

Jump Up
Jump Up

Two pulled the tree limb down
Down, down to the ground

With it pulled down low
One climbed on to this limb turned bronco

The tree cowboy holding firm
To the nearest branch
Turned bronco mane

Release
"Wheeeeeeeeee"

Bounce, Bounce Bounce ....
And it was over

"My turn now!!!"
Said another.

At Sula's Feet

Watching the Radio

John R. from Nash...ville.... Tenn-e-ssee
We miss you.

We sat for hours watching you on the radio
We dared not move
For we had waited a better part of the evening
For the radio signal
To grow strong enough
For you to come to visit

You had such power in your voice
You had such warmth in your voice
You had such joy in your voice

You were such a friend

Who were you anyway?

Ersula Knox Odom

Junie Johnnie

Leola Sula Roberta
"Our Rock"

Louis Margaret

My Support System

~ Support System ~

Ersula Knox Odom

Inspiration Is In The Room

Inspiration just walked in
Sat down next to you
Smiled at you a moment ago
Shook your hand during the meet and great
Nodded in agreement when you shared your idea
Reminded you of the time when something wonderful happened
Reminded you of the lessoned learned a while ago
Caused you to think about what you just said

Dusted off a dream deferred and gave it life

Inspiration just stood up for another is in need
You barely noticed for motivation has you by the shoulder

Your feeling of euphoria is beginning to carry you
What a wonderful light spirited feeling it is
You are ready
You tell someone about your idea and as you do
Inspiration sits down
beside that person

At Sula's Feet

Bible Under My Pillow

When did she tell me
When did I first realize it worked
When did I tell my children
Why do they know it works

What subconscious skill
Could read while I slept
To transfer the knowledge
That the words written within
Would keep us
From all hurt, harm and danger

Ursula Knox Odom

Discipline 1- "Spank Her"

As the preacher began
You talked, whined, and then cried

Aunt Janie Said
"Take her outside and spank her"
I protested
She repeated

"Take-her-outside and spank her"
I did

And it worked
From that day forward
All I had to say was
"You wanna go out side"
You said "No ma'am"

Now people say
"You have such a well mannered daughter"

I smile and think to myself
It only took one trip outside

At Sula's Feet

Discipline 2 - "The Agreement"

Too old to spank you
So I screamed at you
All in your face

Then
You laughed

I inquired
Have you lost you last mind?

You replied
"Ma, with you screaming like that
and your hair like that
You look like a lion"

We laughed

I explained that when you ....
Then I ....
Let's agree that you won't ....
Then I won't ....

We agreed

Ursula Knox Odom

Church on Sunday?

Which church depended on which Sunday

First Sunday
We went to the Baptist church

Second Sunday
We went to the Methodist church

On Friday night
We went to the Sanctified church

For God was everywhere

At Sula's Feet

Good Bye, Auntie

They say the sons
Suffer for the sins of the father

I now know that daughters are protected
By the graces of the mother

Your smile and goodwill created a desire
for others to protect all that you cherished

Your loved ones
Your memories
Your legacy

Your child is protected
By the sweet words that others whisper to her

Your memory is protected by the joy that we feel
As we see you in our mind's eye
As we speak warmly of you

Your legacy lives in the nieces
Who promise to be like you for the rest of their days

Even in your pain the nurses said:
"She's funny and she' s sweet."
The doctors exhausted their powers to save you
For they knew You were special

You asked God to hold your hand and He did
For He knew best and He led you home to rest

Ursula Knox Odom

Mentally Ill Mom

Mother's Hell
Child's purgatory

Child:
> Afraid to love her for
> the veil of shame will follow

Mother:
> Dreams lost
> the beautiful voice
> the unequaled intelligence
>
> Gone

Child:
> Fear— will it happen to me

Mother:
> How can I protect this child
> from the horrors I've faced..
> I was a home economist..
> She's heading that way...

Child:
> I won!!!!
> All packed and ready to go to state..
> OH NO!!
> She hide my materials
> The team left without me.
>
> I hate her!

At Sula's Feet

> I can't hate her!
> she can't help it., she can't help it, she can't help it.

Mother:
> I can't stand my sister
> for my child loves her more
> I resent my mother
> for my child loves her more

Mother:
> This is my child
> There is nothing else real in my life

Child:
> Goodness Gracious
> Why does she stare at me so?

Adult child:
> She took care of me for 9 months
> I've taken care of her for 96 months
> I must learn to love her.

Adult child:
> She's really a nice person
> She's really a lovable person
> She's really a funny person
> I actually love her
> what a wonder
> I was never her baby
> but now she is mine

Mother:
> What can I ask her to bring to me
> yet it is her that I want to see.

Ersula Knox Odom

Nice Words

The words you said were exactly what I needed to hear
When I needed to hear them

They inspired me
They enlighten me
They amused me
They gave me courage to go on

I'm sorry they did not benefit you.

At Sula's Feet

Nosey Neighbor

On this day
A boy dared venture to my house
Yes he got lost
And had to ask his way
In this strange place

He had dirt roads to brave
Even before coming face to face
With my horror
I now had to tell Grandmama he "liked" me

He had barely said "hello"
When at the door Miss Ada knocked
"I just wanted to see eho that boy was
I was sending down here"

Ersula Knox Odom

Oh The Shame of It All

One Friday night after a bit too much to drink
Uncle Louis said to me
"You want to know how to have a baby?"
"I'll show you how to have a baby"

I could not believe these words
Came from my dear Uncle Louis

He went on to say that he

"was tired of seeing my head
Buried in those _____ magazines
If you have to do something
Watch the soap operas
But don't listen to the ___it they say
See how they dress
See how they set the table.."

It's amazing how much true love
Can come from such
An embarrassing moment

At Sula's Feet

98

Outcast's Companion

You did simple things
I saw the good in you

You said stupid things
I saw the good in you

You embarrassed me
I saw the good in you

Then you saw the good in me

Even though we have not spoken
Many times over the years
We both know that
We created a comfortable
Spot for each others' soul to rest

When others tossed it about

Ursula Knox Odom

Secrets

My My

Somebody better talk to those chillin'

This one's talking to his sister
And doesn't know it

That one's kissing his cousin
And doesn't know it

It's a shame that
Everyone knows but that child

She took that secret to her grave

Lord have Mercy!

At Sula's Feet

The Baby Child

I was the
Baby child
Of the baby child
Of the baby child

Child......
I heard stories
Of many generations

Ursula Knox Odom

The Sanctified Church

Tambourine
Washboard
Tap
Clap
Drum

At Sula's Feet

"Luv Ya!"

I rolled it around in my mouth
And liked the taste of it

I stroked it
And liked the feel of it

I tried it on for size
And it fit

"Luv Ya" he said

Yep the friendship was born

Ersula Knox Odom

My Father's Name

Hey little boy with my father's name

It's decided
I like you no matter what

No matter what you say
No matter what you do

You are the first evidence
That Walter is not just a picture

Even though little boys meant
Nothing to me in first grade
You got my attention
And held it for life

You have no last name
You have no face

You are just
Walter from the first grade

At Sula's Feet

My Mother's Name

I gave you my mother's name

When she got to heaven
She talked to the angels about you

My brothers love you
My child with their mother's name

"Hey Niecie" they say
"You gon have the family reunion
At your house this year"

They want to call Mama's name again
And sing and dance again
Laugh again

I am happy
That you are my gift

We are thrilled
That you did not disgrace the name

We are overjoyed
That we get to love you
Without shame
Without excuses

You are wonderful
And we want to tell the world
About you.

Ursula Knox Odom

At Sula's Feet

~ Final Thoughts ~

Ersula Knox Odom

Brain Washing

I think
> Brown is the color of dirt

You know
> All life spring from the earth

I think
> Black cat
> Wandering Jew
> African Violet
>> Bring bad luck

You know
> Luck is what I believe
> And this is your subtle way
> of making me believe I am bad

I think
> I can sprint
> I can't run cross country

You know Cross country is a way of life for Africans

I think
> I can't sing opera

You know
> Leotyne Pricc better than I do

I think
> Dark skin is bad

At Sula's Feet

You know
> It's God's gift of eternal youth
> You risk your life to fake it

I used to think
> I couldn't play tennis
> I couldn't play basketball
> I couldn't play football
> I couldn't play golf
> I couldn't play baseball

You Know
> I know better than that now
> For I am the greatest - ever

Ursula Knox Odom

Greetings That Matter

Hi Honey
Hi Sweetheart
Hello Wonderful
Hey Baby
Hi Luv
Hello Beautiful
HHHeeeyyy!!!!!!! (With a smile on your face and in your voice)

For those of you
Who hear yourself
In these words

We thank you
We love you
For you make us feel good
About ourselves

At Sula's Feet

That's Life

Happiness, a feeling that Life gives us,
Then snatches it back when we begin to enjoy it.
This makes us sad, but- That's Life

Hatred, a feeling that we return to Life,
When happiness has been taken from us.
She could care less, but-That's Life

Love, a feeling that can bring back that stolen happiness.
Strangely, it can also make us sad and afraid,
Afraid that one of Life's children will
come and take it away again.

When this happens, our hearts, minds,
and souls sink deeper and deeper
Into a dark abyss of self pity, but--That's Life
War, that ugly faced child of Life who comes around
 When happiness and love for our fellowman
 Is nowhere to be found.

We are debauched by him and led to fight,
Or say things that will hurt us and the one we love.
The only reward for our abasement is
The laughter of the evil child, but-That's Life
Yes-That's Life

If she were to change, our minds would be
In a chaotic state, wondering, "What Happened?"
Yes-That's Life

Ersula Knox Odom

Life is A Journey

As we travel along the road
In route to what we feel is our destiny
Lots of people we do meet
In search of harmony
We meet them at the rest stops of our life
Some provide the intellectual
And emotional fuel we need
Some carry us for a while
Some we carry for a while
Some we leave behind

At Sula's Feet

Misunderstood

Some say:
>If you let someone take your picture
>"You let them take your life"

Does it mean:
>That the person dies

Or Could It mean:
>That they allow someone to
>"Take your life"
>To another generation

Some say:
>"You shouldn't let the right hand
>Know what the left hand is doing"

Does it mean:
>Keep secrets
>Or keep your business to yourself

Or Could It mean:
>If fingers from the left hand
>Are interlocked with those of the right hand
>Where each can feel the pulse of the other
>Very little work can get done

Ersula Knox Odom

Motivation

Ribbitt!!
I encourage you

Ribbitt!!
You encourage me

Ribbitt!!
Ribbitt!!

We encourage each other

At Sula's Feet

Selfish

Me

Ersula Knox Odom

Sweet Potato Bank 2

Potato "Bank"?
We did deposit them at harvest time
We did withdraw them as needed
Because we saved some during times of plenty
We did have them when others went empty.

At Sula's Feet

You Folks

You folks?!!
What ever do you mean
Is that the same as you people

Don't like that either

Do you not see me

Have I melted into
A collage of nameless faces
When did I lose my individuality

Stop
Look at ME
Ask ME what you want to know

Stop
Look at ME
Tell ME what you want ME to know

Else
Go write a speech and talk to the masses
Because I've got to go talk
To someone who knows I'm there

Ersula Knox Odom

Baby Shower

This new generation
Pulled a fast one on us
They had men at the shower
That stayed in the room
For all the criticism
We cast upon them
And all the gloom
And sorry for their tomorrow
They got it right
This party was planned
And successfully executed by friends
A man and a woman
Who invited and encouraged
Men and women to attend
Some knew the mother-to-be
Others did not
It was simply a network of friends
Coming together
To enjoy each other's company
And reminisce
Coming together
To support friends

At Sula's Feet

Who cared about
A mother-to-be
Since a man and a women
Played the create the baby game
Men and women were allowed to play
The welcome the baby game
Men can laugh and act silly too
It just sounds a little different
In the end
It truly was a celebration
Of a new life
New friendships
New inclusion of
Fathers and uncles

Ersula Knox Odom

Born With It

Last Night I heard a storyteller say:
"Our bodies remembers Africa"

My goodness.... I hope this is true

To think that I can reach within my soul
To find spiritual gold designed to make me whole

To touch Africa

Get back to great great grandma
Because the richness of her home terrains
Ran in her veins

If animals can miraculously learn to do
As their ancestors have done without being taught
Then our bodies are drawn to the wisdom and knowledge
Of our ancestors without being taught

That one drop of blood carries the memories
That centuries can not erase

At Sula's Feet

Our lack of conscious knowledge about our heritage
Is like a sleeping lion, while unaware the power is still there

What my eyes see and my body knows often don't agree
Some say I carry myself like a queen
I say: " oh no this cannot be" but they say: " it is so"

So from Eve to me, from Cleopatra to me
From Queen of Sheba to me, I am one with our history

To support our innate abilities
As our love ones braided our hair
They revived those code words of pride and
Weaved them in with each twist

Quiet Code words like:

"you so precious"
"you're a blessed child"
"you can do anything you put your mind to"
"you're an old soul"
"this child's been here before"

Ersula Knox Odom

Enjoy your journey!

At Sula's Feet

About the Author

Born in NC and raised in rural GA by the maternal grandmother for whom she was named, Ersula Knox Odom's first dalliance as a "life lyricist" began with a poem that she penned at age seventeen in response to a poem that her boyfriend had written her.

At the age of 18, writing became an important component of her life; her interest in writing and poetry was piqued when she won an award from the Alpha Phi Alpha Fraternity writing contest at Savannah State College. She graduated with honors from Effingham County High and earned a theatre degree from Eckerd College.

The year 2004 proved to be the year that would bring all Ersula's poetry to the forefront to bring *At Sula's Feet*, her recollections and life lyrics based on the experiences of a "country girl" from the dirt roads of Georgia and the wise words (or "witdom" as she calls them) of her grandmother, affectionately known to all who loved her as "Sula."

In addition to writing, Ersula is currently a representative with Primerica Financial Services. She is married with two wonderful daughters, she resides in Tampa, Florida.

Ersula Knox Odom

At Sula's Feet

ORDER FORM

If you would like to order more copies of *At Sula's Feet* photocopy the order form below and mail your order form to:

Sula TOO.com

235 W. BRANDON BLVD, SUITE# 111
BRANDON, FL 33511
1-888-564-SULA (7852)

(PLEASE PRINT)
NAME:_____
ADDRESS: _____
ADDRESS 2: _____
CITY, STATE, ZIP: _____
PHONE: _____

QUANTITY	DESCRIPTION	UNIT	TOTAL
	AT SULA'S FEET - BOOK	14.00	
	AT SULA'S FEET - AUDIO/CD	10.00	
		TAX	
		S/H	5.95
	* ADD $1.00 PER BOOK AFTER TWO BOOKS		
		TOTAL	

METHOD OF PAYMENT
( ) MO ( ) VISA, MASTERCARD, DISCOVER, AMEX (PLEASE CIRLE ONE)